MAKING HISTORY

ROME
in the time *of*
AUGUSTUS

Written by
Fiona Clarke

Illustrated by
Mark Bergin

SIMON & SCHUSTER
YOUNG BOOKS

Contents

INTRODUCTION   3
THE HOME OF A ROMAN NOBLE   4
THE DEATH OF JULIUS CAESAR   6
A TRIUMPHANT RETURN   8
ROME'S GOVERNMENT   10
A VICTORY PARADE   12
THE ARMY   14
RELIGION AND SACRIFICE   16
THE ROMANS' GODS   18
GOVERNING THE EMPIRE   20
THE TEMPLE OF MARS   22
LIFE IN THE CITY   24
HOMES FOR THE RICH, HOMES FOR
   THE POOR   26
GAMES AND GLADIATORS   28
THE DEATH OF AUGUSTUS   30
IMPORTANT DATES   32
INDEX   32

DESIGN: DAVID SALARIYA
EDITOR: PENNY CLARKE
CONSULTANT: FIONA MACDONALD

FIRST PUBLISHED IN ITALY BY
GIUNTI GRUPPO EDITORIALE, FIRENZE
UNDER THE TITLE NELLA ROMA DI AUGUSTO

THIS EDITION FIRST PUBLISHED IN 1993 BY
SIMON & SCHUSTER YOUNG BOOKS
CAMPUS 400
MAYLANDS AVENUE
HEMEL HEMPSTEAD
HERTS HP2 7EZ

ISBN 0 7500 1345 1 (HARDBACK)
ISBN 0 7500 1346 0 (PAPERBACK)

PRINTED IN ITALY BY GIUNTI INDUSTRIE GRAFICHE

Introduction

THIS BOOK DESCRIBES THE LIFE of the people of Rome during the time of their ruler Augustus. Augustus, one of the greatest of all Roman rulers, was born in Rome on 23 September 63 BC and died at Nola, near Naples in southern Italy, on 19 August AD 14.

He was actually called Caius Octavius Caesar, and is often referred to in history books as Octavian. The change of name to Augustus was a sign of the enormous respect the Roman people had for him. The Senate voted to give him the title 'Augustus' on 16 January 27 BC. It was the first time the title had ever been given to a human being, before that date it had only ever been used in a religious way.

However, it was probably not so surprising that the Romans thought Augustus was like a god. After years of civil war he had given them peace. After the dangerous manner in which Julius Caesar changed the governing of Rome and its empire (page 6), Augustus had restored the traditional, balanced way of government.

The people of Rome lived at the centre of a rich, stable empire, thanks to Augustus's skill and efficiency as head of state or, to use the term the Romans themselves used, 'the principal citizen'. As principal citizen Augustus was the most powerful man in the world, because, when he lived, the Roman Empire and the known world were almost the same.

It was an extraordinarily difficult task for one man to be ruler of so great an empire, to keep all its peoples prosperous and at peace, and to make sure that government and the law were tolerant, fair and efficient. Through intelligence, courage, determination and immense hard work, Augustus succeeded in this almost impossible task.

The Home of a Roman Noble

WEALTHY ROMANS ENJOYED A HIGH standard of living, with a large house in Rome and an estate in the country.

This Roman noble clearly lives on one of the hills around Rome, away from the city's summer heat and dust. It doesn't matter to him if his home is not close to the city centre because he can afford horses, either to ride into the city or to take him there in a light carriage. Poorer people needed to be within walking distance of everything they needed, such as work, markets and friends. This man's friends are as wealthy as he, and can afford their own transport.

Most Roman noblemen were also senators, members of the Senate, the ruling council of Rome, so they usually had a constant stream of visitors. They came to ask favours, discuss new laws or chat about the Roman army's latest successes abroad.

The entrance hall of the house often served as a reception area for the visitors. Simply furnished, the master of the house reclined on a couch, while everyone else stood.

MB

The floor of this entrance hall is made up of different coloured marbles. Such floors were a status symbol among wealthy Romans. This pattern is made up of quite large pieces of marble. Other types of floor, called mosaics, were made up of tiny pieces of coloured stone laid out in elaborate patterns or pictures. Some of these floors still survive.

The master of the house and the boy (perhaps his son) and the two visitors are all wearing togas. These were the formal dress of all Roman citizens – men who were not slaves. Made of wool, they were worn over a tunic and were uncomfortably hot in summer. When he became Emperor, Augustus usually wore a toga of rough home-spun cloth woven by his wife.

The Death of Julius Caesar

THE ILLUSTRATION ON THESE TWO pages is a reconstruction of a very famous murder: the murder of Julius Caesar on 15 March, 44 BC.

Julius Caesar was the great-uncle of Augustus and the most powerful man in Rome. He became dictator in 48 BC and was elected dictator for life in 44 BC. He was popular with the people and a successful military leader. The Roman Empire increased enormously while he was in power, and the city of Rome itself became wealthier than ever.

△ The Senate had granted Julius Caesar the right to wear a purple toga. Purple was the symbol of imperial power, so only a very powerful head of state could wear it. This sign of Caesar's power alarmed many people. It also made his enemies more jealous than ever. The purple dye for the toga came from shellfish and was very expensive because many hundreds were needed to get even a small amount of dye.

It was easy for the senators plotting Julius Caesar's death to hide the murder weapons — long thin daggers — in the loose folds of their togas or in the parchment scrolls that any busy senator might carry.

Julius Caesar was stabbed to death in the Senate at the foot of a statue of Pompey, whom he had finally defeated after a long power struggle only four years earlier, in AD 48.

MB

So why was Julius Caesar murdered? Traditionally, the Senate was Rome's governing council, so its members, the senators, were important and powerful men. (No woman could be a member of the Senate.) However, as Julius Caesar's success and popularity increased, he ignored the Senate and government officials, taking more and more power into his own hands. Finally, he became dictator. This caused fear and jealousy among the senators, for although he had many supporters, he also had many enemies. Among them were Brutus and Cassius, his chief political rivals. It was they who plotted Julius Caesar's murder.

A Triumphant Return

JULIUS CAESAR'S MURDER THREATENED ROME with civil war, as his enemies and supporters struggled for power. Knowing this might happen when he died, he had made a will naming Augustus as his adopted son and the next ruler of Rome.

Augustus heard this news in Greece, where Julius Caesar had sent him to finish his education. As the new ruler of Rome it was his duty to punish his great-uncle's murderers. But he had to be careful. Many powerful senators thought like Brutus and Cassius and did not want an inexperienced young man as their ruler.

Augustus, however, had his own supporters. Marcus Antonius was the most powerful and together they hunted down Brutus and Cassius. But they soon quarrelled and for the next thirteen years Marcus Antonius fought Augustus. Marcus Antonius had the wealth of Egypt behind him, because he and Cleopatra, the Queen of Egypt, had fallen in love. Finally, in 31 BC, at the battle of Actium, Agustus defeated the forces of Marcus Antonius and Cleopatra, who both committed suicide.

The war was over, his enemies were dead and Augustus returned to Rome in triumph.

▽ Like his great-uncle before him, Augustus celebrated his victory over his enemies with a great triumphal procession through the streets of Rome. Crowds thronged to marvel at the amazing things in the procession: golden statues of gods and goddesses quite different to their own, carried by prisoners-of-war who would be sold as slaves, and gold treasure by the cart-load.

△ Of course the most important person in the procession was Augustus. He drove a magnificent chariot. Behind him in the chariot stood a slave holding a wreath of laurel leaves above Augustus's head. Laurel wreaths were symbols of victory.

△ Close behind Augustus's chariot came two strange-looking objects. These were the bows (fronts) of two of Marcus Antonius's ships captured by the Romans at the battle of Actium. The bows symbolized the broken power of the enemy.

9

Rome's Government

Traditionally, Rome had been ruled by two consuls, together with representatives of the ordinary people and some junior officials. The consuls were elected each year from the Senate – a system deliberately designed to stop one man becoming too powerful.

Julius Caesar had ignored this system. Augustus, however, preferred the old ways, which won him the support of many of his great-uncle's enemies. This popularity had its dangers. By 23 BC Augustus had been elected consul each year since 31 BC. Realising he was in danger of losing people's support, he resigned.

Four years later, faced by war and starvation, the Senate elected Augustus Consul for life. Although this went against all their traditions of government, the Romans had realized just how much they needed his wisdom and political skills.

From then (19 BC) until his death in AD 14, Augustus was the real ruler of Rome. Other consuls were elected to work with him, but no laws were passed or important decisions made without his agreement. He sat as a judge in the law courts. He also worked hard to get rid of corrupt and lazy senators. In Julius Caesar's time the Senate had 900 members, Augustus reduced the number to 600.

MB

▽ Augustus restored the power of the Senate in the government of Rome and the Roman Empire. During debates any senator could say what he liked without fear of punishment, although Augustus did introduce time limits for speeches, so that everyone could have a turn.

▽ Senators were entitled to wear a purple stripe on their tunics or togas as a sign of their status. They also enjoyed special privileges, such as reserved seats at the public games. But although important, they could not leave Italy without getting permission from the Senate.

11

A Victory Parade

THE POWER OF ROME DEPENDED on its army, and it was a superb army. The Roman legions, the army's fighting units, were famed and feared for their bravery and skill in war.

The soldiers came from all over the Roman Empire. Led by young noblemen and experienced officers, known as centurions, the army was a well-trained, highly disciplined fighting machine. Like his great-uncle Julius Caesar, Augustus was a brilliant general and his troops adored him. They helped him conquer many new territories. Rome needed these territories for their wealth and the taxes they had to pay. Without grain from Spain and Egypt, many Romans would have starved.

At the end of every successful campaign there was always a great victory parade through the streets of Rome. The legions which had fought in the campaign paraded in all their splendour before the Emperor. Their commander led the way on horseback, followed by the legion's standard-bearer. Behind marched the rest of the victorious troops.

Sometimes, as part of the victory procession, the ruler of the defeated country had to walk through the streets in chains, to symbolize Rome's power. This was why Marcus Antonius and Cleopatra committed suicide after the battle of Actium. They were determined not to suffer such a humiliation.

MB

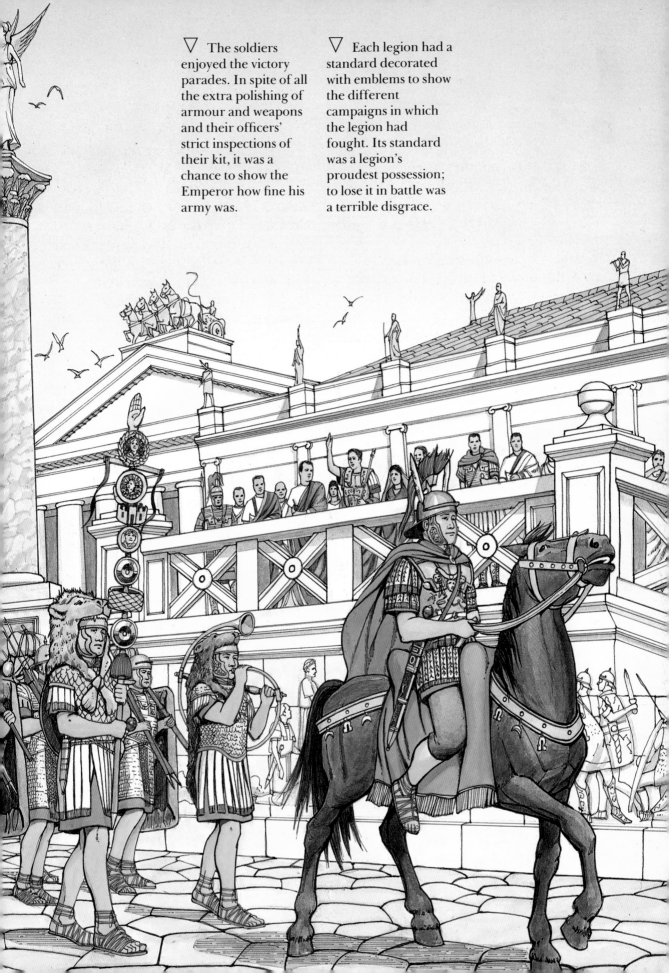

▽ The soldiers
enjoyed the victory
parades. In spite of all
the extra polishing of
armour and weapons
and their officers'
strict inspections of
their kit, it was a
chance to show the
Emperor how fine his
army was.

▽ Each legion had a
standard decorated
with emblems to show
the different
campaigns in which
the legion had
fought. Its standard
was a legion's
proudest possession;
to lose it in battle was
a terrible disgrace.

The Army

AUGUSTUS CREATED
A PERMANENT PROFESSIONAL
army always ready for action. The core
of this army was 28 legions, each made
up of about 4000 men. Soldiers signed
on for a set period: 16 years at first, and
then 20. They were paid a salary,
although over half went to pay for
food, clothing, weapons and armour.

Augustus also established an
elite force, the praetorian guard. He
kept about 3000 of these troops
permanently stationed in Rome, ready
to defend the city in any emergency.

The Roman Empire was so
large it needed extra troops to help in
local trouble-spots. These soldiers came
from the different countries of the
Roman Empire and fought with their
own local weapons, such as bows and
arrows or sling-shots. They also formed
most of the army's cavalry, because the
Romans were poor horsemen.

Traditionally, these extra
troops were sent home when they were
not needed. Augustus realised that this
was inefficient and dangerous.
Inefficient because all the training was
wasted once the troops were dismissed;
dangerous because these men had had
military training and were armed, so
could just as easily attack the Romans as
defend their empire.

GERMANY

FRANCE

SPAIN

ITALY

GREECE

NORTH AFRICA

MEDITERRANEAN SEA

BLACK SEA

ASIA (MODERN TURKEY)

EGYPT

ROMAN EMPIRE IN THE TIME OF AUGUSTUS 27 BC

AUGUSTUS'S CONQUESTS 27 BC TO AD 14

STATES ALLIED TO OR PAYING TAXES TO ROME

1. A Roman soldier in full armour. His weapons are a sword, a spear and a dagger.
2. The 'tortoise', a defensive formation of 27 soldiers.

3. Siege towers were mounted on rollers and pushed up to the walls of towns under siege so the soldiers in the tower could get over the walls.

4. A giant battering ram to destroy walls.
5. A scorpion, a catapult for throwing small rocks.
6. Onagers were used to hurl huge rocks.

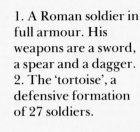

7. The legion's trumpeter wore a bear's skin over his helmet, armour and the rest of his uniform.

8. Carrying the legion's standard was a very great honour. Only the bravest soldiers were allowed to do so.

9. Each centurion commanded a hundred men.
10. The camp prefect looked after all the legion's kit.

11. The tribune was a legion's second officer.
12. Every legion was commanded by a legate.

Religion and Sacrifice

THE ROMANS WORSHIPPED MANY DIFFERENT gods and goddesses, each one concerned with a different aspect of life, such as love, war or the weather. They also believed there were many invisible spirits, some kindly, some evil. To encourage the friendly spirits to work for you meant offering food and wine to the gods, keeping holy days and religious festivals and giving thanks when things were going well.

Most families kept a small altar in their home. There they prayed to the guardian spirits of the house, to the spirits of their country and to the spirits of their ancestors.

Towns and cities throughout the Roman Empire had public temples and altars, where priests made sacrifices to the gods, to ask them for their blessing. In Rome's early days, human sacrifices had been common, but by Augustus's time animals and birds were killed instead.

In 12 BC Augustus was elected Chief Priest, along with all his other titles and honours. Being Chief Priest meant that he played an important part in the main religious ceremonies. Many people believed he was specially favoured by the gods and built altars to his 'genius' or guardian spirit. Augustus tried to stop this – he knew he was human, just like his subjects.

▷ When he was elected Chief Priest in 12 BC, Augustus had to take part in the sacrifice of animals to the gods at the many religious festivals. At the most important festivals many animals were sacrificed and at least one was a great white bull. To sacrifice a bull meant that the person making the sacrifice was showing the god, or goddess, great respect, because a full-grown bull was an expensive animal.

▷ The Romans often made gods of their rulers – once they had died. When the emperor Vespasian, who lived about sixty years after Augustus, was very ill towards the end of his life his friends asked how he was feeling. In reply he joked: 'I feel I am becoming a god.' The Romans also believed in fortune-tellers. One told Julius Caesar to 'Beware the Ides (15th) of March.' He was killed on that day.

The Romans' Gods

THE MOST POWERFUL OF THE Romans' gods was Jupiter. They believed he ruled over all the other gods and goddesses. Jupiter's weapon was a thunderbolt and he was feared rather than loved. His wife, Juno, was a complete contrast. She brought peace and prosperity and was worshipped as the queen of heaven.

Less powerful than the gods, but also important, were local spirits who lived in rivers, woods and trees.

Other mysterious gods were worshipped by the conquered tribes who lived in distant parts of the Empire. Some of these, like Isis in Egypt, or Mithras from Persia, attracted many followers among the Romans. Although Augustus disapproved, Mithras became extremely popular with the Roman troops because he promised strength in battle and life after death.

1. Apollo, god of the sun and light.
2. Juno, Jupiter's wife and goddess of women and children.
3. Jupiter, the chief of the gods.
4. Diana, goddess of the moon and hunting.
5. Victoria helped give success in war.
6. Janus, the god with two faces.
7. Minerva, goddess of wisdom.
8. Asclepius, god of health and doctors.
9. The symbol of the sun god.
10. Mercury, the gods' winged messenger.
11. Venus, goddess of love and beauty.
12. Mars, god of war.
13. The Lares, spirits of the land.
14. Mithras the Persian sun god could only be worshipped by men.

15. Nereids, water nymphs who lived in freshwater as well as in the sea.

16. Tritons, sea gods with the heads and bodies of men and the tails of fish.

17. Neptune, god of the sea and the waves.
18. Amphitrite, wife of Neptune.

19. Sirens, sea nymphs with beautiful voices, lured men to their deaths.

20. Bacchus, the god of wine and good living.
21. Ariadne, the wife of Bacchus.

22. Satyrs, gods of the country.

23. Ceres, goddess of the harvest.
24. Fauns, male spirits of the countryside.

25. Nymphs, tree spirits.
26, 27. Pan and Flora, guardians of the country.

28. The Furies, ugly evil spirits.
29. Cerberus, the three-headed dog, sat at the door of Hades (Hell).

30. Pluto, god of the dead.
31. Persephone, wife of Pluto and goddess of spring and new life.

32. Charon, the mysterious boat-man who ferried the souls of the dead across the river Styx to Hades.

33. Somnus and Mors, gods of sleep and death.
34. The Gorgons, hideous monsters, symbols of terror.

19

Governing the Empire

AUGUSTUS TRAVELLED WIDELY THROUGHOUT THE Roman Empire but he could not, of course, govern it all himself – it was far too large. He governed about half the provinces – the regions into which the empire was divided – and appointed deputies to help him while he was away. The rest of the provinces were under the control of governors, usually appointed by Augustus.

The governors were experienced politicians and diplomats. They had served in the Senate and held office as consul, so they knew how to govern efficiently. Although a governor was the emperor's representative in a province, he had a great deal of power, and the farther from Rome the province, the greater the governor's power. Communications were only as fast as a horse could gallop or a boat sail, so orders from Rome could take weeks to reach provinces like Britain or what, today, we know as Lebanon.

Applying the laws made in Rome, dealing with the ruler of the conquered territory and collecting taxes were the governor's most important duties. Augustus wanted to reform taxation and ordered a census, or population count, throughout the empire. It is mentioned in the New Testament of the Christian Bible, because that is why Joseph and Mary had to travel to Bethlehem.

▽ Paying taxes is never popular – a fact Augustus understood very well. He was keen to raise as much money as possible, as efficiently as possible. To do this he needed to know how many people lived in the lands ruled by Rome. So he ordered a census, or count, of the population. This was an enormous undertaking and had not been done before. Each governor organized the census in his own province.

▽ If there was any danger of trouble in a province, perhaps because the day for paying taxes was approaching, there were always plenty of loyal Roman soldiers around to make sure everything went well.

Governors were usually wealthy men anyway, but they always became richer. The local merchants found it useful to be friends with the governor – which meant giving him money and presents.

21

The Temple of Mars

AUGUSTUS WAS A VERY RICH man. His family was wealthy and as the governor of many provinces he became even richer. He spent a great deal of his own money on magnificent public buildings in Rome and other cities throughout the Empire. As an old man he often joked that when he arrived in Rome after Julius Caesar's murder it was a city of brick, but now it was a city of marble!

The Temple of Mars the Avenger was one of the buildings Augustus paid for. He had promised to make this offering to the gods once he had tracked down his great-uncle's murderers.

▽ Augustus's building projects made Rome the finest city of the time. Most of the men who worked on the buildings were slaves, prisoners-of-war captured on military campaigns. The work was hard and many died, but, to the Romans, the life of a slave, especially one who had been an enemy, did not matter. There were accidents, as there was no machinery to lift the stone.

▽ Getting all the building stone to the site took time, especially when the site was in Rome, like the Temple of Mars and the Forum. Wooden carts pulled by oxen were the only form of transport.

▽ Augustus tried to preserve old Roman customs, so he banned anyone not wearing a traditional toga from entering his new Forum. Togas were so hot in summer that this was most unpopular.

When the Temple of Mars the Avenger was finished, Augustus used it as his military headquarters – Mars was the god of war. After a successful campaign, the victorious legions made a special procession to the temple to offer their weapons to the gods.

The temple dominated another of Augustus's magnificent schemes: the new forum, or public meeting place, in the centre of Rome. Here, under the colonnades, away from the hot summer sun and the driving winter rain, the people of Rome could meet to shop and gossip. They could also admire their emperor's generosity – just as he intended!

Life in the City

THIS IS HOW MOST ROMANS lived. What a contrast to the nobleman's country house on page 4 and his town house on page 26.

As the capital of the Roman Empire, Rome grew fast. People came to live there from the countryside and the Roman provinces overseas. It became almost impossible to house everyone. To solve the problem Roman landlords built large blocks of flats, which they let out, a room at a time, to families desperate for somewhere to live.

These flats were noisy, draughty and smelly. The people who lived in them could not afford a proper water supply or good drains. Instead they had to carry their water in from the street and store it in huge pottery jars. Many districts had clean, hygienic public lavatories, but it was not always convenient to use them – especially at night.

Fire was a constant danger. People used small portable stoves for cooking and heating the flats, and it was all too easy for stray sparks or falling embers to set the flimsy wooden floors alight. It is hardly surprising that many Roman men spent most of their time out of doors, buying and selling, setting up workshops beside the streets, or just talking and drinking with friends.

▽ The crowded flats and streets of the poor districts of Rome were unhealthy places to live. Many babies died from diseases caused by pollution and overcrowding. Others were abandoned by parents too poor to be able to bring them up. Dumping babies, especially girls, on the nearest rubbish heap was quite legal and very common. Some might be rescued, but most of them died.

▷ As a result of the census (page 20), Augustus knew that about a million people lived in Rome. He also knew that the overcrowded, unhealthy slum districts should be improved. He made many efforts to reform local government, to make it more efficient at keeping Rome clean and safe. He successfully set up a local police force and a local fire-fighting service, both popular measures among the poor who lived in the slums of Rome.

MB

Homes for the Rich, Homes for the Poor

1. Entrance hall
2. Door guard's room
3. Main hall (atrium)
4. Living room
5. Main bedroom
6. The family's rooms
7. Main reception room
8. Bed from Pompeii
9. Bedroom cupboard
10. Greek-style chair
11. Portable heater for liquids
12. The back door
13. Shops
14. Servant's room

△ Only a wealthy man could afford to live in a house like this. It would have had richly painted walls and mosaic floors (page 5). In the courtyard was a small garden and a fountain. The hall or atrium, which also had a pool, was where the family received their friends and visitors. It had very little furniture.

▷ A very large number of people lived in this block of slum flats. There was no garden or fountain in the courtyard of these flats, just a well from which everyone had to get their water, carrying it up to their rooms. Many flats did not even have wells, so people had to carry water even further.

26

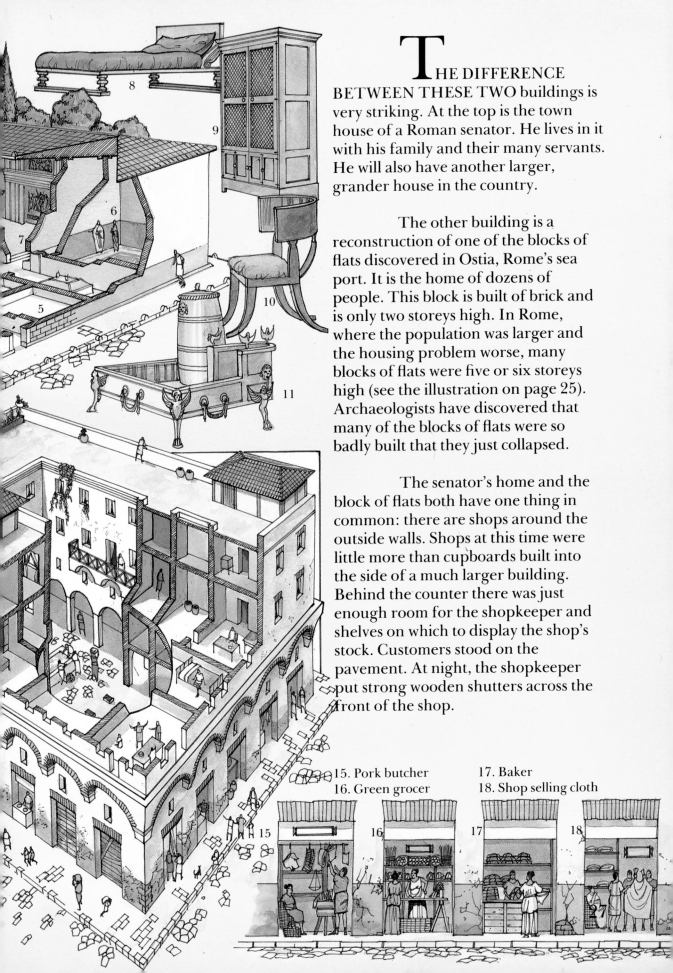

THE DIFFERENCE BETWEEN THESE TWO buildings is very striking. At the top is the town house of a Roman senator. He lives in it with his family and their many servants. He will also have another larger, grander house in the country.

The other building is a reconstruction of one of the blocks of flats discovered in Ostia, Rome's sea port. It is the home of dozens of people. This block is built of brick and is only two storeys high. In Rome, where the population was larger and the housing problem worse, many blocks of flats were five or six storeys high (see the illustration on page 25). Archaeologists have discovered that many of the blocks of flats were so badly built that they just collapsed.

The senator's home and the block of flats both have one thing in common: there are shops around the outside walls. Shops at this time were little more than cupboards built into the side of a much larger building. Behind the counter there was just enough room for the shopkeeper and shelves on which to display the shop's stock. Customers stood on the pavement. At night, the shopkeeper put strong wooden shutters across the front of the shop.

15. Pork butcher
16. Green grocer
17. Baker
18. Shop selling cloth

Games and Gladiators

▽ Men fighting wild animals was always popular with the crowds who flocked to watch the public games. Although the animals were extremely fierce they seldom killed the armed men, the gladiators, sent to fight them because they were not free to charge their attackers. They were shackled to heavy wood or stone blocks.

Men fighting other men was another popular event. Once again the fight was not equal because the gladiators were armed in different ways. One might have a net and a short sword, so he would have to get close to his opponent, who might have a spear and a shield so he could attack from a safer distance.

If one man got the other on the ground, the emperor decided if the defeated man should die. A thumbs up signal and the man lived, but if it was thumbs down, the man was killed on the spot to a great cheer from the crowd.

THE ENTERTAINMENTS THE ROMANS ENJOYED most were the great public games. Originally these had formed part of some religious festivals, but, by Augustus's time, they were just entertainments. Because the people enjoyed them so much, putting on public games was a good way for the wealthy to gain popularity. There were always games to celebrate successful military campaigns. These were usually paid for by the army commanders out of the enemy's treasures they had captured during the war.

One of the first things Augustus did when he reached Rome after Julius Caesar's death was to organize a magnificent public games. This was a deliberate attempt to win popularity.

Today we would find many of the events in the games extremely cruel and shocking. Some Romans thought so too, but they were a minority. Most leading Romans believed that it was good for the crowds to let off steam at the games, baying for the deaths of men and frightened wild animals. If they didn't have this outlet of controlled violence, there might be uncontrolled violence against their rulers.

The Death of Augustus

'AFTER TWENTY YEARS THE CIVIL wars were ended, foreign wars buried, peace recalled . . . force was restored to the laws, authority to the courts and majesty to the senate . . . Ploughing returned to the fields, honour to religion, security to men, and a peaceful possession of property to each individual.' This excellent summary of Augustus's achievements was made at the time of his death, aged 77, in AD 14.

What was the secret of Augustus's success? First and probably most important, he was loyal to friends, who, in turn, were loyal to him. He and his closest political allies, Agrippa and Maecenus, remained friends throughout their lives.

Augustus worked hard – and expected everyone else to do so too. He could be brave and generous, but he was also cautious, calculating and secretive. He lived simply, so no enemy could be jealous of his wealth and luxurious way of life.

He like the old, traditional ways and although he was an extremely clever politician, he did not want power for its own sake. He so clearly worked for the good of Rome and not himself that it was difficult for people who disagreed with him to whip up anger against him.

Sadly for Rome, the rulers who followed Augustus had few of his skills.

30

When Augustus died in AD 14 he had ruled the Roman Empire for 58 years. Most of the people had never known any other ruler, so his death meant a time of sadness and uncertainty. He was buried in a great mausoleum (a huge tomb rather like a temple) that he had had built many years earlier. His funeral procession was the longest Rome had ever seen.

Even as an old man, Augustus was as efficient and well-organized as ever. In his will he listed all the military and financial resources of the empire that he had ruled for so long.

On 17 September, a month after his death, the Senate declared that Augustus was a god. Today we still remember him from the month that had been given his name: August.

31

Important Dates

BC
63   23 September, birth of Caius Octavius
Caesar – Augustus
48   Julius Caesar defeats Pompey
Murder of Pompey
Julius Caesar becomes dictator
44   Julius Caesar becomes dictator for life
44   15 March, murder of Julius Caesar
31   Caius Octavius Caesar elected Consul for
the first time
Battle of Actium, defeat of Marcus
Antonius and Cleopatra
27   16 January, the Senate votes Caius
Octavius Caesar the title of Augustus
23   Augustus resigns as Consul

19   The Senate elects Augustus Consul for
life
12   Augustus elected Chief Priest
AD
14   19 August, death of Augustus

The initials 'BC' stand for 'Before Christ' and indicate events that occurred before he was born. 'AD' indicates events that occurred after Christ's birth.

Index

A

Actium, battle of 8, 9, 12
army 4, 12, 13, 14; *see also* soldiers *and* weapons
Augustus 3, 5, 6, 8, 9, 10, 11, 12, 14, 16, 18, 20, 21, 22, 23, 24, 29, 30–31

B

Brutus 7, 8

C

Caius Octavius Caesar *see* Augustus
Cassius 7, 8
cavalry 14
centurions 12, 15
Cleopatra 8, 12
clothes 5, 11; *see also* togas
consuls 10, 20

E

Egypt 12, 18

F

food 12
furniture 4, 26

G

gladiators 28–29
gods 16, 18–19
governors 18, 21, 22

H

houses 4, 24–25, 26–27

I

Isis 18

L

laws 10, 20
legions 12, 13, 14, 15, 23

M

Marcus Antonius 8, 9, 12
Mithras 18
mosaics 5, 26

O

Ostia 27

P

Persia 18
Pompey 6
praetorian guard 14
provinces 20, 21, 22, 24
public games 11, 28–29

R

religion 16–17, 18–19, 29
Rome 4, 8, 9, 10, 11, 12, 14, 16, 20, 21, 22, 23, 24, 27, 29, 30, 31

S

Senate, the 3, 4, 7, 10, 11, 20, 31
senators 6, 27
shops 27
slaves 5, 9, 23
soldiers 14, 15, 21; *see also* army *and* weapons
Spain 12

T

taxes 12, 20, 21
Temple of Mars 22–23
temples 16, 22–23
togas 5, 6, 7, 11, 23
transport 4, 23

V

Vespasian 16

W

weapons 14, 15, 23, 28